Paula
Happy 20

love
John

Golden Days

GOLDEN DAYS

Favorite Moments
To Cherish and Share
Written by
Edward Cunningham
Illustrated by
Tracy Jones

HALLMARK EDITIONS

Golden Days

What makes a golden day?
A bright, sunny day
Filled with fun things to do,
A day when it's wonderful
Just to be you?...

Holidays are golden days...
They can be make-a-new-start days,

And warm heart-to-heart days.

Turkey days are golden days...

So are bunny days...

And wear-something-funny days!

There are golden days
for firecracker popping...

And golden days
for last-minute-shopping!

But what of all your other days?
Just stop and think a minute...
Doesn't every single one
Have something golden in it?

Some big thing?

Some small thing?

Some nice-to-recall thing?

Maybe it's something fun...
Like splashing in the sun,

Or hearing a catchy new melody,

Or noticing for the very first time

How red a rose can be.

It could be something nice you do...

Like writing a long, newsy letter,

Or paying a visit to someone dear...
That would even be better!

Perhaps it's

Something lazy...

Like an afternoon you spend

Taking it easy

With your favorite friend!

Your something golden
Might be as warm as a kiss,

Or a just-between-us smile,

Or going for a walk
With someone you like
And dreaming a little while...

Many things are golden,
And each in its own way
Can help to brighten up your world
And make a golden day...

So if you always look for gold
In the things you say and do,
Every day you live can be
A golden day for you!